T0001462

SAY YES to Yourself

50+ UPLIFTING LESSONS IN SELF-EMPOWERMENT, SELF-CONFIDENCE, AND SELF-WORTH

MOLLY BURFORD

Adams Media
New York London Toronto Sydney New Delhi

▲adamsmedia

Adams Media
An Imprint of Simon & Schuster, Inc.
57 Littlefield Street
Avon, Massachusetts 02322

First Adams Media hardcover edition November 2020

ADAMS MEDIA and colophon are trademarks of Simon & Schuster.

For information about special discounts for bulk purchases, please contact Simon & Schuster Special Sales at 1-866-506-1949 or business@simonandschuster.com.

The Simon & Schuster Speakers Bureau can bring authors to your live event. For more information or to book an event contact the Simon & Schuster Speakers Bureau at 1-866-248-3049 or visit our website at www.simonspeakers.com.

Interior design and illustrations by Priscilla Yuen
Interior images © 123RF/elenarolau, fastfun23

Manufactured in the United States of America

10 9 8 7 6 5 4 3 2 1

Library of Congress Cataloging-in-Publication Data
Names: Burford, Molly, author.
Title: Say yes to yourself / Molly Burford.
Description: Avon, Massachusetts: Adams Media, 2020. | Includes index.
Identifiers: LCCN 2020034536 | ISBN 9781507214411 (hc) | ISBN 9781507214428 (ebook)
Subjects: LCSH: Self-confidence. | Self-esteem. | Self-realization.
Classification: LCC BF575.S39 B865 2020 | DDC 158.1--dc23
LC record available at https://lccn.loc.gov/2020034536

ISBN 978-1-5072-1441-1
ISBN 978-1-5072-1442-8 (ebook)

This book is dedicated to my father, Chris,
who has always encouraged me to look at everything my sisters
and I offer with pride, confidence, and compassion.

TABLE OF CONTENTS

INTRODUCTION

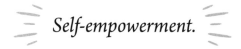

Self-empowerment.

You've likely heard the term before, and it's no surprise: It's a concept that is fundamental for living your very best life. After all, to feel empowered in your own skin means taking the reins and steering your future in the direction you want to go—the direction that will lead you to success and happiness.

You are capable and worthy of living the life you want and loving yourself. Sometimes you just need a reminder! And that's what *Say Yes to Yourself* is all about.

Here you will discover dozens of important lessons, interactive exercises, and inspirational quotes to help you manifest—and maintain—self-esteem, confidence, and a sense of empowerment.

In the pages that follow, you'll:

REWRITE THE STORY YOU TELL YOURSELF

LEARN TO TRUST THE TIMING OF YOUR OWN LIFE

PRACTICE POSITIVE AFFIRMATIONS

MAKE A SELF-EMPOWERMENT PLAYLIST

FALL IN LOVE WITH YOUR POTENTIAL

FOCUS ON YOUR STRENGTHS

AND MORE!

You can read this book beginning to end or flip through to lessons that are most helpful for a current situation. But before jumping in, be sure to check out the following section for how to use this book. There you will uncover tips for making the most of all this book has to offer. It's time to start saying yes to yourself—and hello to the joyful, fulfilling life you were always meant to live!

HOW TO USE THIS BOOK

Are you seeking to feel more confident in your everyday life? Maybe you've begun to doubt yourself or have never really felt capable of achieving your dreams. Whatever the case, this book is here to help you show up to your life every day with self-assurance, excitement, and courage. The more than fifty lessons that follow offer direction, clarity, inspiration, and practice for saying yes to yourself. And what does it mean to say yes to yourself, exactly? Saying yes means having faith in who you are and showing up to your life each day as your authentic self. It's giving yourself permission to live the life you want to live.

Using this book is simple and straightforward. Keep it nearby and pick it up whenever you start to doubt your awesome self. You can flip to a lesson that is pertinent to your present challenge, or simply read it straight through for inspiration. Some lessons will provide activities you can complete right away. Others offer mindsets for you to carry through life. There are also quotes from driven, self-empowered individuals who have done the work to trust themselves and their lives. Manifest their energy so you can watch your world expand and your confidence grow! You can keep this book on your bedside table to read before bed or on your coffee table to pick up when the moment strikes. It's even small enough to take on the go.

Most importantly, take these lessons in with an open mind and heart. You will need to unlearn the old lessons that made you doubt yourself in the first place. You will also need to tune out the harmful voices—from yourself or others—that have told you that you had to be everything and anything but yourself. *You* are enough. You are more than enough. You already have all the power within you to not only do what you want, but also what you need and are meant to do. Sometimes, you just need a little guidance.

Now let's get started! ∂∆

WORK WITH WHAT YOU'VE GOT

You are totally full of potential! You just need to tap in to the right parts of yourself and work with what you've got. Not a morning person but thrive in the afternoon? Use that to your advantage and schedule your most important meetings and tasks for noon onward whenever possible. Hate running but love going for hikes? Stop forcing yourself to get on the treadmill and find hiking trails for exercise. Whatever your situation may be, it just comes down to being realistic and self-aware. You're perfectly fine the way you are. Really—you are! The trick is to focus on your strengths, not your weaknesses.

Focus on your *strengths*,
not your weaknesses.
Focus on your *character*,
not your reputation.
Focus on your *blessings*,
not your misfortunes.

ROY T. BENNETT, author

MAKE A SELF-EMPOWERMENT PLAYLIST

Music can deeply affect your mood and attitude. In times of stress or insecurity, pop on a self-empowerment playlist to turn that negativity into inner confidence. Have your playlist readily available on your phone or computer so when a difficult situation or self-doubt strikes, the likes of Lizzo will remind you that you are *100 percent…* you know the lyrics.

Need some inspiration for your own playlist? The following are some empowering song suggestions to get you started.

"FEELING MYSELF"
by **NICKI MINAJ** and **BEYONCÉ**

"EVERYTHING I AM"
by **KANYE WEST**

"BORN THIS WAY"
by **LADY GAGA**

"ROAR"
by **KATY PERRY**

"THE WAY I AM"
by **INGRID MICHAELSON**

Design Your Empowering Environment

Whether you live alone, with roommates, or with a significant other, your home is a reflection of, well, you! Make sure your space is not only inspiring but functional and helps you live your best life. Keep rooms tidy and your things easy to find with baskets and drawer organizers. Frame inspirational quotes to keep you motivated. Find trinkets that remind you of happy times. There are tons of *YouTube* videos out there with design ideas, organizational hacks, and more that will help you organize and decorate your unique space in ways that make sense for you.

IT'S YOUR LIFE—

DESIGN IT WELL.

BOBBY BERK,
Queer Eye interior designer

Do More of What You're Not Great At

You can't be good at everything immediately, and nothing builds confidence like learning a skill and working to improve it! It's also a great way to practice a little self-discipline, which will come in handy whenever you are faced with a more difficult task in the future. Whether it's dancing, getting into home renovation, or public speaking, be kind to yourself and allow yourself to be less-than-amazing at something new. Exercise the beginner's mind! To get the ball rolling, consider making a list of some things you aren't totally great at. Pick one thing from that list to pursue today.

PRACTICE SAYING NO

When an event comes up that you're sincerely not interested in going to, or you are already maxed out for time, say no in a gracious way to the person who is asking you for your time and energy. For example: *I appreciate the invitation, but unfortunately I can't today. I hope you have a great time!* It can feel uncomfortable at first, but in time it'll become easier, and it is an important part of respecting your own needs and wants.

Thanks so much, but I'm completely tapped for time. Please ask me again in the future, though! Sounds fun.

I love you, but it's not my thing. I appreciate you thinking of me, though.

Thanks for the invite, but I have a few things that need my attention first.

Volunteer

Volunteering reminds you that there's so much more to this life than yourself, helping you to take a break from thinking (i.e., worrying) about yourself and focus on someone or something else. It also affirms that you can make a difference in lives other than your own, which is powerful stuff! You could go to an animal shelter, work at a soup kitchen, or spend time at a nursing home. Take a break from worrying about your life and improve the lives of others.

Even if you just change one life,
you've changed the world forever.

MIKE SATTERFIELD, pastor and founder
of Field of Grace Ministries

Try Daily Positive Affirmations

Positive affirmations are a fantastic way to manifest confidence. When you repeatedly tell yourself something, you really won't have a choice but to believe it! Each morning, go to a mirror and repeat one of the positive affirmation suggestions on the following page. You can even write these affirmations (or a few of your own design) on sticky notes and put them in places you will see them regularly so you're reminded often of what an amazing person you truly are.

I am worthy.

I am smart and capable of handling my life.

I trust the universe has my back.

I have faith in myself.

I am loved.

CREATE A CUSTOMIZED SELF-CARE ROUTINE

Self-care is all the rage—and for good reason. It is about nurturing yourself—body, mind, and spirit—through deliberate, loving acts of care. Instead of always running on empty as you focus on doing more and being more, you make time for things that recharge your batteries and manifest more health and happiness. It's important to develop a self-care routine that makes sense for you and your lifestyle. What may work for your best friend may not work for you, and vice versa—and that's okay! For example, maybe your friend recharges after a long day at work by spending time with family, while you need quality "me time" to feel refreshed after your shift. Make sure you check all the boxes you need to feel like the most empowered, nurtured version of yourself.

BE YOUR OWN BEST FRIEND

The person you spend the most time with is you. Every day—every minute—you are with yourself. And you also have the most say over how you feel about yourself. So why not be your own best friend? Take yourself out to dinner; go for a solo walk around town; have fun with yourself like you would a close friend. And speak kindly to yourself every day, just like you would to a friend. You wouldn't belittle a friend for their haircut, would you? Be nice to yourself! Practicing positive self-talk and spending quality time with just you are great ways to better your relationship with yourself and cultivate a greater appreciation for who you are.

Instead of Saying I'm Sorry, Say Thank You

When you're late—whether you're meeting a friend for lunch or turning in a project—find a way to say *thank you* instead of *I'm sorry*. This way you show that you care without putting yourself down in the process. *Thank you for waiting for me. I've been looking forward to our visit! Thank you for your patience as we work on this project. I'll have the report in by Friday.* When you decide to speak about yourself with respect and kindness rather than belittlement and cruelty, you are showing yourself you have a choice in how you treat yourself and that you deserve to be treated well. You are showing up for yourself as your own compassionate friend. Think about past situations where you've apologized. How might those *I'm sorry* phrases be turned into *thank you* phrases?

INSTEAD OF:

SAY:

"I'm sorry I'm late." "Thank you for being patient."

"I'm sorry you have to help with this." "Thank you for helping out."

"I'm sorry you had to cancel your other plans." "Thank you for being there for me in a time of need."

"I'm sorry I didn't know how to do this." "Thank you for showing me the ropes."

Acknowledge the Negative Voice Inside of You

To hear negative or self-defeating thoughts is not a sign that you should change course—that you're a failure or completely crazy. It's an indication that you are venturing into uncharted territory. It is new and exciting…but also scary. Instead of thinking of the inner voice as cruel, think of it as an older sibling or parent figure trying to protect you: It has good intentions in trying to keep you in the realm of everything known. Acknowledge and thank that voice for trying to protect you, then let it go. This is your life, and you are in control.

Talk to yourself like
you would to someone
you love.

BRENÉ BROWN,
author and social worker

Set Boundaries

Setting boundaries for yourself is absolutely crucial to your well-being. They are the very foundation of self-respect and protect you from emotional and physical burnout. Some examples of healthy boundaries include saying no to invitations when you need to recharge, not allowing others to go through your personal property, and answering emails and phone calls on a schedule that works for you. How do you know what your own boundaries are? Begin by noticing when something bothers you about someone's behavior. What did they do, and why do you think it affected you? Determine whether this behavior is a quirk that you can overlook or something that will continue to impact your relationship with that person in a negative way. It's not always comfortable to say no, but when you say no to others based on your needs, you're saying yes to yourself.

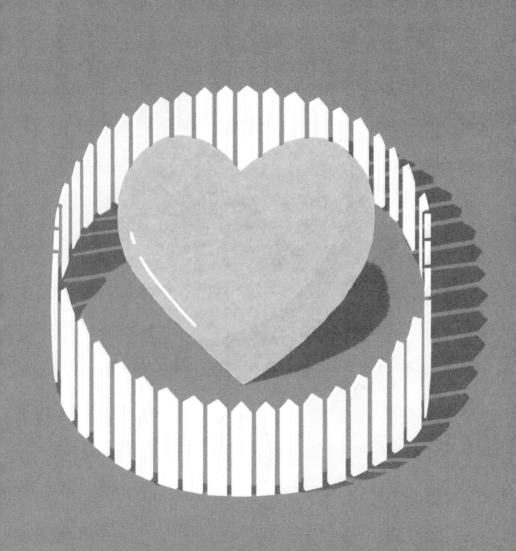

INVEST IN YOURSELF

You are your biggest investment. You wake up with yourself in the morning and go to sleep with yourself at night. Only you are responsible for you. And that's pretty empowering stuff! Why? It's all up to you to decide how you want to live. Everything you need rests within your own hands. Embrace this responsibility and invest in yourself. Make doctor appointments. Exercise. Eat right. Watch your emotional energy. You are your everything; never forget that.

Invest time and energy in your well-being. Create an atmosphere of emotional safety for yourself.

AMY LEIGH MERCREE, author

Accept Compliments Without a Disclaimer

You deserve praise, congratulations, and admiration! When someone compliments you, accept their kind words and your accomplishment by offering a simple thanks. Leave the *but* out of it. *Thanks...but* (*Thanks...but I didn't really contribute that much. Thanks...but I still have 10 pounds to lose.*) lessens your power and questions the judgment of the person who complimented you.

PRACTICE MINDFUL SOCIAL MEDIA

Social media is a world that touches almost every part of your life. Seriously. Promotion at work? Share that accomplishment on *Facebook*. Good hair day? Send that selfie over *Snapchat*. Weird shower thought? Tweet it, *obviously*. Remember: You are both the curator *and* the patron of your online life. You choose what you post as well as what content you consume. So, be mindful of whom you follow and only fill your feeds with accounts that inspire you and bring you joy (and those belonging to people you know and love IRL). Most importantly, be careful of the comparison trap. When scrolling through *Instagram*, for example, be mindful of when you start to compare your home, body, social life, etc. to someone else's, and redirect your thoughts to a more self-empowered stance.

Don't compare your life to others'. You have no idea what their journey is all about.

REGINA BRETT, author

CREATE A
FIVE-YEAR VISION

Notice that this is a vision, not a plan. The reason for this is that plans can sometimes lead you to act rigidly in your life. They don't necessarily promote flexibility or account for the ways you might change in the years to come. In life, you're meant to evolve and grow! Having said that, there are some primary aspirations you probably *are* going to continuously aim for, such as health, happiness, loving relationships, and a solid career. Consider writing down the categories (career, friendship, health, etc.) you envision as being pivotal to your ideal future in five years. For each category, brainstorm ways you will achieve them. To build a solid career, for example, you might regularly commit to learning new skills for your trade. And remember to adjust your vision as needed!

FOCUS ON THE WHY

When you're working toward realizing your full potential and becoming more empowered, do your best to remember why you began this journey in the first place. Think of how being more confident will positively impact your life and the lives of those around you. Observe all the ways insecurity and self-doubt may be holding you back. These will both contribute to your why. Whenever you start slipping into negative self-talk or bad habits, remind yourself why you started this journey. It will become that much easier to keep going!

REMEMBER

WHY YOU STARTED.

Unknown

Challenge Yourself

Feeling challenged by something doesn't mean you won't ever overcome it or master it. It simply means you're pushing out of your comfort zone and trying something new! A great way to build confidence is by showing yourself all that you're capable of. Whether it's trying a new lift at the gym, learning a different language, or kicking a habit that no longer serves you, don't be afraid to challenge yourself. Consider some ways you can challenge yourself. Try one of these things today!

Explore Your Values (and Live by Them)

Sometimes you might feel disempowered when you realize you aren't living life according to what you truly believe in. Maybe you love spending time with family and friends but are too focused on work to pay them much mind. Or perhaps you value good physical health but have been skipping regular exercise or eating poorly. When you ignore your values, you ignore yourself. It's a form of self-betrayal because you are abandoning what makes you who you are in favor of things that obscure your true self. Luckily, you can always start again! Try writing out your values on a piece of paper. How might you not be abiding by one or more of these beliefs? How will you live life according to these important values moving forward?

ROMANCE

FRIENDSHIP

HONESTY

COMPASSION

LOYALTY

COURAGE

ADVENTURE

WORK YOUR BODY

Show love for your body—and give yourself a little reminder of the wonderful things it can do—by working out. It's so easy to get caught up in negative body image, especially when you're inundated with images of "perfect" bodies everywhere you turn. But every body is amazing in its own unique ways. Rediscover what is amazing about yours! Consider what exercises you enjoy and make you feel good. Try to include at least one of these exercises in your weekly schedule, not with the sole aim of changing how you look, but to promote health and feel powerful.

Dodge the Productivity Trap

The working world puts an emphasis on productivity that can often lead to burnout when left unchecked. Long workweeks, crazy deadlines, and the rat race may leave you gasping for air. But there is more to life than work. You are allowed to take breaks, disconnect during the weekend and after hours, and create a balance between your professional and personal worlds. Make sure you're making time for all those other important pieces of your life too. When is the last time you took a long shower or bath? Or hung out with friends (without checking your email)? By making time for what's important to you, you are giving yourself permission to focus on what life is really about. Think about activities you love but haven't pursued lately. Try including one of these activities in your schedule for the week.

BE YOUR OWN
ROLE MODEL

There are tons of worthy role models to look up to, but how about yourself? Think of how you could act in a way that would make your younger self proud. Think of who you wanted to be when you were younger and look at what you're currently doing to be that human. You will probably find you're already most of the way there!

Act as if what you do
makes a difference.
It does.

WILLIAM JAMES,
philosopher and psychologist

HOLD SPACE FOR ALL OF YOUR EMOTIONS

Allow yourself to feel all that you do. Don't "should" on yourself, as the saying goes—*I should feel this way; I shouldn't be upset about that.* Instead, honor what you feel, including the tough emotions like jealousy, anger, and sadness. The reason this will help you feel more empowered is because you are quite literally giving yourself permission to not only feel what you truly do, but to regulate your emotions so they don't build up inside and eventually boil over (often when you least want them to). What do you think you "shouldn't" be feeling? What might you say to that self-doubting voice to affirm it's okay to feel this way?

MANAGE YOUR LIFE

You are the manager of your own life. While tons of events will occur that are totally out of your control, how you respond to and make do with what happens *is*. This shouldn't scare you, though; if anything, this should lead you to feel more empowered! You are capable. Still not convinced? That's okay! Try this mindset to help you out: Think of life as an unruly subordinate at an office where you are the boss. Think of ways you can work with—rather than against—its disruptive behavior. Don't be afraid to get creative!

Act As If You're Already Who You Want to Be

On the journey to getting to where you want to be, it's easy to get discouraged or sidetracked, or, worst of all, to abandon the mission altogether. Sometimes, throwing in the towel is the result of fear—fear of failure or fear that you will look dumb for even trying. Other times, it's simply because of frustration—that it's taking longer than you thought it would. So what's the solution? Act as though you're already the person you want to be! Think about that future self and imagine their habits, daily routines, and mindsets. What do they do each day? Who do they surround themselves with? Now implement those behaviors in the present. Prove to yourself that you can be who you want to be by acting like that person today.

You must become the

producer,

director, &

actor

in the unfolding
story of your life.

WAYNE W. DYER, author and motivational speaker

Replace Negative Self-Talk

Negative self-talk is detrimental to your self-esteem. When you frequently think or say hurtful things like *I always screw things up* or *I could never achieve that*, you're eventually going to believe them. And over time, these words can even become self-fulfilling prophecies, leaving you more disempowered. Positive self-talk, on the other hand—kind words such as *I can learn from this* or *I am capable of whatever I put my mind to*—fosters self-empowerment and love for who you are. In fact, research into athletic performance has shown that practicing more positive self-talk is an indicator of greater success in personal and professional pursuits. So what are you waiting for? Let's get positive!

INSTEAD OF:	TRY THIS:
I always mess everything up!	I made a mistake, but I can learn something from it!
I could never do that. I'm not good enough for that job.	If I put my mind to it, I can do that job.
Why am I so stupid?	I am feeling challenged, but that doesn't mean I'm stupid.
Ugh, why did I make that mistake?	I made a mistake, but it doesn't define me.

REWRITE YOUR NARRATIVE

Perhaps you've been feeling down and out because of something that happened in your past—something that sparked self-doubt and left you decidedly disempowered. That experience is shaping your future as you carry those heavy memories and emotions with you from one day to the next. Well, it doesn't have to! You can rewrite your narrative. This is your story, after all, and no one can tell it better than, well, you! What story are you currently telling yourself? How might it be keeping you from truly accepting and loving who you are? Now rewrite it! Tell it the way it's meant to be told: empowering, liberating, and true to you.

Once upon a time...

Ask How Could I Not?

Instead of thinking *How could I?*, ask yourself *How could I not?* Whether you're considering going for that promotion, asking someone out on a date, or pursuing some personal goal, ask yourself how you couldn't go for it. How could you pass up this opportunity? As the saying goes, even if you miss the moon, you land among the stars! Even if things don't work out as you had hoped, you took the chance—own that power. Maybe something even better than you imagined comes of the experience. Think about times when you have asked whether you could or should go for something you wanted. How might you change that *How could I?* into *How could I not?*

Trust the Timing of Your Life

Feeling like you aren't where you "should" be in life? Comparing your relationship status or career to a friend's? The truth is life has different plans for everyone. No one has the same journey (how boring would that be?). Try your best to set aside society's milestones—the different events like getting married, buying a house, making X amount by the time you turn forty—that are painted as one-size-fits-all standards everyone should follow. Instead, live according to your own goals, aspirations, and wants. Trust that as you focus on what feels right for you at each part of your unique journey through life, everything will happen as it should.

Don't compare your chapter one to someone's chapter twenty.

Unknown

DRESS FOR THE LIFE YOU WANT

Don't wait for the life you want to show up at your doorstep to look the part; dress for it as if it's already here! Show up every day as if you are already leading that best life. Wear that crop top to the beach. Rock those heels at the club. Throw on a fabulous pantsuit and strut into the office like you are in charge. The way you dress is a reflection of yourself. Show the world who you want to be. Dress up as that person, and eventually you will become that person!

TRY BODY POSITIVITY AFFIRMATIONS

Body positivity is about not only accepting your body as it is but also celebrating all that it does for you. Of course, it's easy to get caught up in what you think you "should" look like or what you "could" look like. However, by doing that, you're missing out on the present and all that you already are! It can be hard to rewrite your narrative when it comes to something as personal as your body, but body positive affirmations are an easy way to get you started. When you start to notice those pesky, unkind thoughts cropping up, replace them with something positive about your body. It may seem forced at first, but with repeated practice, you will feel more confident in your own skin. Try out the following examples or brainstorm your own.

I am worthy at any size.

I am beautiful.

I respect my body.

I am so lucky my body
lets me _____.

I am deserving of love
just as I am.

CREATE A MOOD BOARD

It's difficult to get anywhere if you don't know where you're going. And while life doesn't provide a map, it does provide clues to where you might want to be in the future. Provide yourself with some extra guidance and motivation by grabbing a cork board or piece of blank paper and creating a mood board. Pin or paste anything and everything that inspires you: quotes, goals, trackers—whatever you want!

Explore new plac with friends
self-love
Set an exercise routine
GOALS
PEACE
CALM
SKYPE FAMILY
READ MORE
LOVE
Start to P off Deb
Be kind to yourself

Reach Your Career Goals with These Tips

While work isn't everything, it can be an important part of what makes you feel happy and fulfilled! And if you want to reach your career goals (whatever they may be) a little bit of planning is necessary to get started or stay the course. The following are tips to help you figure out what you want out of your professional life and exactly how to get there.

What do you want your ideal "last" position to look like?

Consider writing down this position, along with what elements factor in to this ideal (having a certain number of employees who work for you, being able to work remotely, etc.).

Now, break up that main goal into smaller steps.

What will it take to get there? If you are a bit confused as
to the necessary steps, try spending some time researching
the role online.

Find a career role model.

They don't have to be someone you know personally, but finding
someone you admire in your field can be totally inspiring (and help
you better understand what you need to do to reach your own goal).

Get to work.

Follow your steps and use your role model as motivation.

Commit to continuous learning.

Most fields are always evolving. Whether it's a seminar or a quick
YouTube video explaining a new development, keep tabs on your
industry shifts (and grow with them).

CHECK YOUR POSTURE

Are you slouching right now? Do you look down at your feet while you walk? Are your shoulders slumped forward? When it comes to self-esteem, posture matters! In fact, research has shown that the way you hold yourself physically translates to how you feel about yourself. The better your posture, the more confident you feel. So, check your posture regularly. If you notice your shoulders are rolled up near your neck, pull 'em back. If you are looking to the ground as you walk, raise your head to look forward.

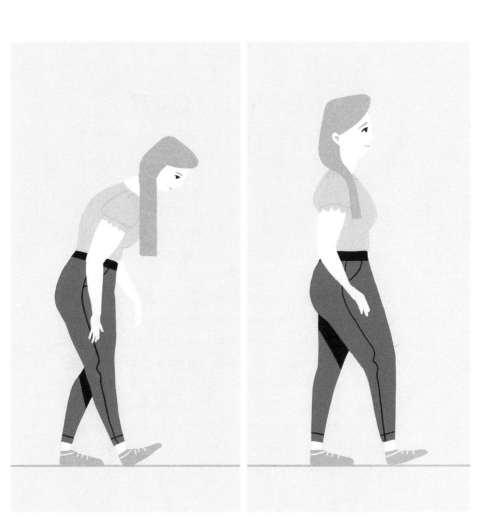

REROUTE YOUR PATTERNS

Human beings are creatures of habit. We all fall into our own routines, whether at work or in our free time. Of course, these behavior patterns can also include the not-so-beneficial, such as eating poorly when upset or defaulting to negative self-talk when faced with an unanticipated challenge. You know yourself better than anyone else, and with that knowledge you can actually reroute negative patterns and get back on the path of self-love and confidence. For example, if you realize stress makes you eat a whole bag of chips in one sitting, keep carrots or other healthy snacks on hand instead. Or perhaps you know that your day always starts off better when you get an extra fifteen minutes of sleep. So be it! When you reroute unhealthy patterns, you make choices that make you feel good about your life *and* yourself.

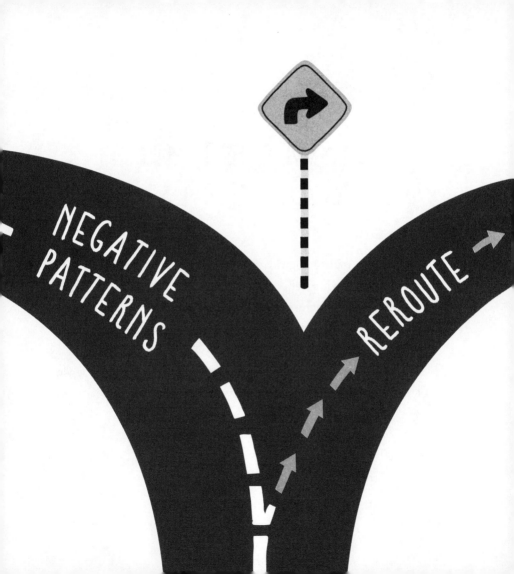

Be S.M.A.R.T. with Your Goals!

Developed by management consultant Peter Drucker, S.M.A.R.T. is an acronym used to help you reach your goals. It stands for: Specific, Measurable, Achievable, Relevant, and Time-Based. Your goals should follow each of these five guidelines. Goals that adhere to the S.M.A.R.T. system help you get to where you want to go, and achieving goals raises your self-esteem and gives you a greater sense of empowerment because it shows you that you can get what you want.

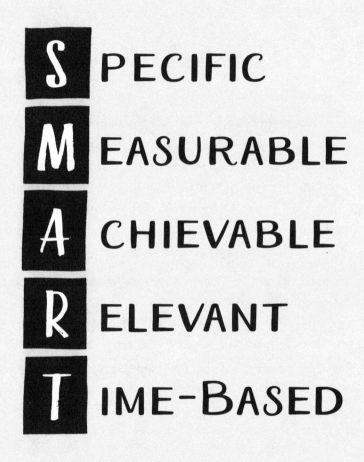

Strike a Pose

Have you ever heard of a "power pose"? Coined by American psychologist and motivational speaker Amy Cuddy, a power pose is an open, strong stance that has been linked to greater self-confidence. The idea is that holding a powerful stance for even just two minutes makes you *feel* powerful. Other people also respond to this display of confidence, reinforcing a more self-assured perception of yourself. There are a number of power poses you can try, including:

The Wonder Woman: Place your hands on your hips and stand with your feet hip-width apart.

The CEO: When sitting, rest one arm on the back of your chair and recline slightly, keeping your knees apart.

The Performer: Stand with your feet slightly apart and hold your arms above your head in a "V" shape.

The Loomer: When standing at a table, plant your hands on the table surface and lean forward.

Don't fake it 'till
you make it.
Fake it 'till
you become.

AMY CUDDY, social psychologist and
author of *Presence: Bringing Your Boldest Self to
Your Biggest Challenges*

UNDERSTAND IT DOESN'T GET EASIER (YOU GET BETTER)

Life doesn't get easier, but you do become better at handling all the obstacles it throws your way. Experience grants you that! Just think about all the hardships you thought you'd never overcome and did. The skills you thought you'd never have (or may not have even recognized) but built over time. Ever gone through a bad breakup? Maybe you learned how to enjoy being on your own. Have you lost a job before? Perhaps you put your networking skills to the test in order to get your career back on track. Try listing your own triumphs and any skills or lessons that came from them on a separate piece of paper. Use this list as a reminder that you hold more power than you often give yourself credit for.

Remember: Perfection Doesn't Exist

Perfection sounds lovely in theory, but it's important to remember that it doesn't exist in real life. Nor should you want to be perfect. The little imperfections are what open up your soul to new and wonderful experiences. They are what allow you to grow and adapt through life's twists and turns. You don't get to stand back up after a fall. You don't get the chance to learn from a mistake. You don't take a risk and reap the rewards of doing something differently. Besides, perfection is boring. There is no room for individuality or expansion in what is perfect. Embrace your own unique imperfections.

I don't know a perfect person.
I only know flawed people
who are still worth loving.

JOHN GREEN,
author of *The Fault in Our Stars*

Fall In Love with Your Potential

When you fall in love with your potential, you fall in love with yourself. You are full of infinite possibilities! You could start your own business. You could create a home that feels like you. You could write that novel you've always had inside. Think of everything you're striving toward—all the different goals you want to reach. Instead of being intimidated by the work involved, be excited by it. Curious, even! Show love for your own potential the way you'd show love for someone else: nurturing it, paying close attention, behaving compassionately, and committing yourself. Be prepared to watch yourself bloom. You hold the watering can, after all! What is one thing you can nurture within yourself today? Your creativity? Your career ambitions? Feed that potential!

Do Something Alone

Confidence is born when you have faith in yourself to take care of your needs and everything that comes with living an independent life. One of the ways you can build up this belief that you are more than capable is by doing more things alone. Of course, there is nothing wrong with asking for help or company, but there is a certain joy and appreciation to be found when you spend quality time with yourself. It is these moments that really shine a light on your strengths.

THE FOLLOWING ARE SOME ACTIVITIES
YOU CAN CHALLENGE YOURSELF TO TRY SOLO.
TRY COMPLETING MORE THAN ONE THIS WEEK!

Shop for new clothes

Go to the movies

Read

Visit a local coffee shop

Enjoy a meal out

Exercise

LISTEN TO YOUR BODY

Listening to your body means tuning in to and honoring your physical needs. It's a simple but important part of nurturing self-esteem, because it shows respect and love for your body. What might your body be telling you right now? Is your mouth a bit parched? Drink some water. Finding it a little difficult to keep your eyes open? Try a power nap. Stomach growling? Have a snack. Legs feeling restless? Take a walk. Listen to your body's cues and show yourself love by caring for its needs.

Remember, you have been criticizing yourself for years and it hasn't worked. Try approving of yourself and see what happens.

———

LOUISE HAY, author and founder
of Hay House

CHECK THESE TENETS OF A HEALTHY RELATIONSHIP

It's been said that you are who you surround yourself with. The people you spend your time with impact everything from your mood to your values to your sense of love for yourself. This is why cultivating healthy, rewarding relationships is one of the best ways to raise your self-esteem. But what makes a relationship healthy? What criteria should you be seeking in your own connections? The following are important factors to look out for when creating and maintaining healthy relationships with friends, family, and romantic partners.

☑ They respect your boundaries

☑ You enjoy your time together

☑ They nurture your growth

☑ They give support when you
are struggling

☑ You can spend time apart without
feeling insecure or guilty

☑ You can express yourself openly and
honestly with them

Stand Up More Than You Get Knocked Down

It's not about how often you fall, it's about how often you get back up; how often you choose to try again—to keep going even though it may feel tough. Real strength lies in adversity. It's a flower continuing to bloom despite the winter cold. It's you standing up after disappointment. And it's claiming control of your life and your happiness. So, pick yourself up, brush yourself off, and keep at it. Every time you try again, you move closer to success.

Knock me down
NINE TIMES
but I get up
TEN.

CARDI B, rapper

GET CREATIVE

Creative expression, no matter its form, leads you down a path of self-discovery. It shows you what thoughts and emotions you're working with, and helps you sort through and communicate them effectively. Also, it's fun! Pick up some watercolors, some charcoal, or even just a pencil and give it a try. If you don't have time right now, include a creative activity in your schedule for tomorrow or sometime later this week. Express yourself through a little creativity and feel your self-esteem rise.

LEARN SOMETHING NEW

Committing to learning something new is a simple and fun way to boost self-esteem. It could be as simple as a new word or as complex as a new language. It could be a new recipe or new software. You're capable of learning anything you put your mind to! Even just giving it a try cultivates a mindset that helps you continue moving forward in your aspirations. So, get curious and dig deep. There's so much to learn about this world and this life!

self-esteem

/ˈˌself əˈstēm/ • *noun*

A confidence and satisfaction in oneself.

WRITE A LETTER TO YOUR PAST SELF

Writing a letter to your past self is a fantastic way to reflect on your achievements and track just how far you've come. You can even choose a specific year that felt super challenging. Write out all you accomplished despite the fray. What did you do well, and what did you learn from the process? This practice will remind you of how powerful you truly are. How you are able to bounce back from adversity. You are strong, and your history is a testament to this fact! Reread your letter whenever you are in need of a little confidence boost.

THE FUTURE INFLUENCES

THE PRESENT

JUST AS MUCH AS

THE PAST.

FRIEDRICH NIETZSCHE,
philosopher

TRY ONE OF THESE ACTIVITIES TO FEEL MORE EMPOWERED TODAY

1 Commit to completing one challenging task. Prove to yourself you're more than capable of anything you put your mind to.

2 Do that annoying but quick errand you've been putting off for weeks or even months. Clear that mental space for better things.

3 Clean your living space. It doesn't have to be immaculate, but tidying as you go and picking up after yourself is a sign of self-respect.

4 Remind yourself that only you are responsible for you. Treat this duty with the upmost importance and own that control; it is powerful.

Try One of These Activities to Feel More Empowered Tomorrow

1 Try keeping to a scheduled bedtime. Being well-rested is key to feeling good physically *and* mentally the next day.

2 Set yourself up for a successful day: Prep the coffee maker, lay out your clothes, write out your to-do list the night before, etc.

3 Put away electronics at least one hour before bed. Put your phone on Do Not Disturb if it helps!

4 Schedule a calming self-care activity to look forward to each night before bed, such as reading, journaling, or meditating.

5 Reflect on what you did well today and what you might focus on doing well tomorrow.

PRACTICE EMOTIONAL INTELLIGENCE

Emotional intelligence, the ability to recognize and effectively express your feelings, is crucial to becoming your best self. It helps you not only understand your emotions as they happen, but also helps you manage them so they aren't coming out in unhealthy ways. Practicing emotional intelligence makes overwhelming emotions feel less scary and empowers you to let go of what no longer serves you. It also helps you better understand and help others. Looking for further guidance on how to expand and strengthen your own emotional intelligence? Brianna Wiest, Heidi Priebe, and Millennial.Therapist are amazing *Instagram* accounts that discuss all things emotional intelligence. Give them a follow!

$\mathscr{I}$t is very important to understand
that emotional intelligence is
not the opposite of intelligence—
it is not the triumph of heart over head—
it is the unique intersection of both.

DR. DAVID R. CARUSO, psychologist

Breathe In Confidence; Breathe Out Doubt

Take a deep breath in through your nose. As you do so, think about everything you're doing right, everything you've overcome, and all the ways you're seriously awesome. Okay, now breathe out through your mouth. As you breathe out, imagine yourself expelling the negative energy you've been holding on to lately: the self-doubt and self-criticism. Let go of everything that's keeping you from loving your life. Rinse and repeat until you feel better. Breathe in that confidence; breathe out that doubt!

WRITE YOUR INTENTIONS

Intentions keep you on track in your goals and help you make the most of each day. As you live with intent, you are able to enjoy and appreciate the present, rather than always jumping ahead to the future or reliving the past. A great way to ensure you're living with intent is to write out your intentions regularly. These could be intentions for the day, week, or even month. You can also keep a separate journal just for these or keep them in a note on your smartphone.

Jump-start your brainstorming with these examples of positive intentions:

I will strive to do the right thing.

I will do my best with what I have.

I will give myself permission to let go.

I will learn from my mistakes.

I will approach life from a position of growth.

Take Up Space

You deserve to be here. You deserve to take up space in your own life. So, speak up! Use your voice. Be loud when you want to be. Don't be afraid to let yourself be seen and heard. You have so much to offer this world; it would be a shame to let all of those lovely things you hold inside stay within you. Plus, the more you act in a confident way, the more true confidence will grow within. It's a muscle—use it!

Do What Works for You—Not Someone Else

In a world full of self-help and advice articles, books, and speakers, it's easy to get overwhelmed by the plethora of *do this, not that*s. And in some cases, there are universal truths (*be kind to others; don't put yourself down for every little mistake; take care of your mental and physical health*). However, every person is different. What works for one person might not work for someone else. Maybe practicing yoga helps your friend release stress, but it makes you feel *more* stressed. Or forcing yourself into a public speaking situation leads to more feelings of self-doubt or social anxiety, no matter how well the speech might have gone. Do what's right for you, despite what others might say. You know yourself best—trust that.

HOW TO BE SUCCESSFUL:

Focus on your own life.

Unknown

PLAN A PAMPER DAY

Self-care is the pinnacle of self-love. These intentional acts of love help you show yourself that you are worth the time, energy, and attention of being cared for. And what better way to practice a little TLC than to pamper yourself? Plan out a time each week for a short pamper session. It could be a thirty-minute bubble bath, just ten minutes to paint your nails, or relaxing in a face mask while you watch your favorite movie. Whatever pampering looks like to you, carving out space for it regularly shows yourself that you're worth being taken care of. You deserve to put your feet up.

Cut the Excess

Making room for the things you love and that make you feel good about yourself and your life sometimes means cutting the things you don't love so much. Perhaps it's a side gig that's draining your energy, a friendship that only takes and never gives, or material things that only take up space in your home. Identifying the excess in your life and letting it go will boost your mood and make room for all the things that serve you more.

For me,
minimalism has never
been about deprivation.

Rather, minimalism is about
getting rid of life's excess
in favor of the essential.

JOSHUA FIELDS MILLBURN, author of
Minimalism: Live a Meaningful Life

REPLACE JUDGMENT WITH CURIOSITY

I can never do this right. Why am I feeling this way? It's so stupid. It can be so easy to judge yourself harshly for everything. Even without meaning to, a critical thought can crop up, making you feel worse about yourself. But you can stop this cycle! The next time you're judging yourself, try replacing that judgment with curiosity. And what does this mean? If you notice a repeated unhelpful behavior, instead of admonishing yourself, gently ask why you keep engaging in something that isn't serving you. Be curious about the cause of this behavior and how you might make a change. This empowers you to not only fix anything that isn't going right but also to love yourself.

BRAG (A LITTLE)

People often feel embarrassed to talk about their own accomplishments. They worry about seeming egotistical or coming off as "braggy" to others. As a result, they end up hiding their abilities—their unique talents and triumphs and everything that makes them special—not just from other people, but from themselves as well. But you deserve to feel proud of yourself! You deserve to talk about your successes and share the awesome traits and skills that make you, well, you. Sure, you don't want to be someone who *only* talks about themselves, but there is a difference between being overly self-centered and recognizing when you have done something great. Give yourself permission to brag a little.

What I am is good
enough if I would only
be it openly.

CARL ROGERS, psychologist

THINK OF FUTURE YOU

As you move through each day, think of your future self and behave in ways they will thank you for. Self-sabotaging behavior has no place here. (For example, staying up until dawn when you know you have a ton of stuff to do the following day.) Instead, try to do things that help you work toward your goals, promote your health, and secure your mental wellness.

Try brainstorming your current habits and ask whether each one serves you. If the answer is no, consider what you could replace that behavior with to better care for future (and present!) you.

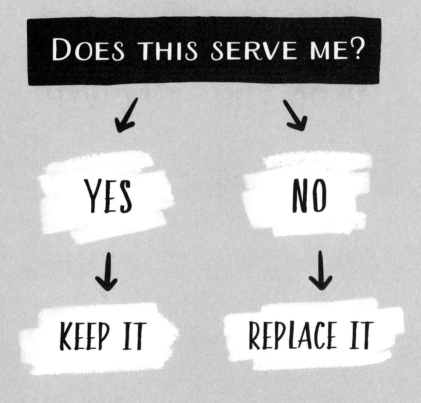

Vlog Your Growth

A fun way to document all the ways you're learning and triumphing in life is by doing vlogs (video blogs). No, you don't have to post these to *YouTube*! However, taping yourself to check in daily, weekly, or monthly is an amazing way to track your progress and truly recognize how capable and downright awesome you are. Also, in the years to come, it'll be fun to look back and see just how far you've progressed. You can even check out video editing software to take your vlogs to the next level.

WORK ON YOU FOR YOU ALONE

When thinking about personal growth and how you might want to improve a skill or shift a part of your life for the better, it's easy to get wrapped up in what others will think about it. Will they be impressed by your new level of physical fitness? Will they understand your career change? But this shouldn't be the driving factor for your own journey to a happy, thriving you! Everyone has different opinions on what success looks like; what matters in your life is what you feel is best for *you*. You need to work on yourself for only yourself. You're the one most impacted by you, after all.

Show Yourself the Love You Give Others

Your love is a magical thing. It heals, brings joy, and comforts others. You should be applying that loveliness to your own self and life too. You deserve it just as much as the world does. You are allowed to bask in your own kindness, your own grace, your own light. Stop being so hard on yourself. Celebrate all that you are—that is love. You are worthy. Never forget that.

You deserve the love
you keep trying to give
everyone else.

BIANCA SPARACINO,
author

CONDUCT A THIRTY-DAY EXPERIMENT

What is a thirty-day experiment, you ask? It is any deliberate change you make for thirty consistent days. It can be as simple as cutting back on your coffee consumption or saving $3 each day. It can also be a larger change, like removing sugar from your diet or working out for thirty minutes each morning. Whatever you choose to do for your own experiment, the purpose is to show you how to approach life with curiosity, intention, and flexibility. It's also to show you that you are more capable than you might think. Make a change and keep at it for thirty days—you might decide to make it a permanent part of your routine!

PRACTICE
MINDSET SHIFTS

Perspective is everything; it dictates how you see the world. If you notice your current way of thinking isn't serving you, perhaps a mindset shift is in order! Cultivating a mindset of growth rather than stagnation, for example, empowers you to keep moving forward in your professional and personal goals instead of getting stuck in a predicament that no longer serves you. A shift from focusing on the negative to seeking out the silver lining can also boost your mood and help you recognize your own abilities. With repeated effort, you can change your life. It all starts with your mind!

MINDSET

IS EVERYTHING.

Unknown

INDEX

ABOUT THE AUTHOR

MOLLY BURFORD is a writer, editor, and social media strategist. She is the author of *The No Worries Workbook*. Her writing has also appeared in *Allure, Teen Vogue, Glamour,* and *Thought Catalog,* among others. Molly was born and raised in Detroit, where she continues to live. She loves her family, friends, all dogs, and pasta. Learn more at MollyBurford.com.